Nw 2-8-85

DATE DUE

MAR 30 1985   MAR 22 1994   MAR 30 2000

MAY 18 1985   JUL 18 1994   AUG 21 2000

JUN 26 1985   FEB 13 1996

JUL 27 1987   MAR 16 1996   AUG 27 2001

FEB 13 1988   AUG 30 1996

MAY 19 1990   FEB 25 1997   DEC 18 2001

SEP 24 1990   MAY 16 1997

DEC 4 1990   OCT 16 1997   JAN 27 2003

SEP 17 1992   JAN 16 1998

OCT -8 1991   JUN 22 1998   NOV 29 2004

                             OCT 02 2006

NOV 19 1991   NOV 17 1998

JAN 21 1992   FEB 13 1999

FEB 12 1992   JUL 24 2012

MAR 10 1992   APR 20 1999   OCT 14 2014

DEC 7   JUN 12 1999

APR 12 1993   JUN 28 1999

              FEB 05 2000

                             OCT 18 2016

                    DEC 06 2014

BRIDGES

BY CASS R. SANDAK

An Easy-Read Modern Wonders Book

FRANKLIN WATTS
New York/London/Toronto/Sydney
1983

Over: the Brooklyn Bridge crosses New York City's East River. It took sixteen years to build and was completed in 1883.

For my father

R.L. 3.7 Spache Revised Formula

Cover photograph courtesy of Redwood Empire Association.

Photographs courtesy of: Michigan Travel Bureau: pp. 4, 22; Virginia State Travel Service: p. 6 (top left); UPI: p. 6 (bottom); Italian Cultural Institute: p. 7; Ewing Galloway: pp. 8, 18 (top and bottom), 20 (bottom left); Chesapeake Bay Bridge-Tunnel Authority: p. 11; New York Thruway: p. 14; New Hampshire Office of Vacation Travel: p. 15; Union Pacific Railroad Company: p. 16 (right); French Government Tourist Office: p. 20 (top); Triborough Bridge and Tunnel Authority: pp. 20 (bottom right), 25 (bottom); New York Public Library: pp. 23, 29 (right); Museum of the City of New York: p. 25 (top left); British Tourist Authority: p. 26 (left); Bettman Archive: pp. 26 (right), 27 (right); the author: pp. 1, 6 (top right), 17, 24, 27 (left), 28 (left and right).

Diagrams by Jane Kendall

Library of Congress Cataloging in Publication Data

Sandak, Cass R.
Bridges.

(An Easy-read modern wonders book)
Includes index.
Summary: Introduces various types of fixed and movable bridges and discusses their construction and uses.
1. Bridges—Juvenile literature. [1. Bridges]
I. Title. II. Series.
TG148.S25 1983   624'.2   83-12522
ISBN 0-531-04624-9

Contents

Bridges to Go from Place to Place

Bridges are structures that help people get from place to place. They also make it easier for animals, cars, trains, trucks, and manufactured goods to go places.

Most bridges cross over bodies of water. Before bridges, the only way to get from one side of a river to the other was by boat or raft—or by swimming! Some cities are built on islands. It would be impossible to walk or drive to them without bridges. Bridges often save many miles on a journey.

Sometimes bridges are built over land. They can be built across valleys and ravines and over roads or railroad tracks. A bridge that goes over land is often called a **viaduct**.

Sometimes a bridge connects one building with another one, or even connects two parts of the same building.

In some places, a bridge made by nature gives a way to cross. Natural Bridge in Virginia is one such bridge formed by water wearing away rock. In the winter, ice sometimes makes a natural bridge where people and animals can cross a body of water.

Steel and cables soar over the roadway of the Mackinac Bridge in northern Michigan, one of the world's longest suspension bridges.

People probably learned to build bridges by seeing what nature had already done. Rivers and streams sometimes have shallow parts where rocks stick up out of the water. People could step from rock to rock to get across the water.

Then people thought of connecting these stones with other stones. Or they put logs between the stones to make crossing easier. These were probably the earliest bridges that people built.

There are many kinds of bridges. And they almost all let people on foot, on bicycles, in cars, buses, trucks, and trains get from place to place quickly and easily.

Thousands of marathon runners jam the Verrazano-Narrows Bridge in New York.

Bridges and Civilization

There is a prehistoric bridge in England called Tarr Steps. No one knows for sure, but it is probably between 10,000 and 25,000 years old. Piles of rock were heaped up to form stone piers. Huge stone slabs **span** the distance between the piers. Tarr Steps is the oldest known bridge structure in the world.

Roman engineers put up strong wooden bridges that could be built quickly and easily. These bridges allowed the legions of the Roman army to advance into new territory and to move quickly in wartime.

In the Middle Ages most bridges built in Europe had gates that could be closed to keep out enemies. These bridges were usually sturdy stone bridges, and they were often lined with houses or shops. One such bridge, the famous London Bridge, lasted for six hundred years.

Built in 1345, the Ponte Vecchio (or "old bridge") crosses Florence's Arno River. Even today it is lined with shops and stalls.

Rivers flow through the heart of many of the world's largest cities, including London, Paris, and Rome. Bridges were necessary to link the settlements that sprang up on both sides of the rivers. These settlements in time grew into large cities tied together by a network of bridges.

As people's needs changed, the kinds of bridges changed. And as people learned about new materials, they learned to build bigger and better bridges.

Bridges are the lifeline of the island of Manhattan—what most people mean when they say New York City. More than a dozen bridges connect Manhattan to surrounding communities and to the rest of the country.

Nine bridges connect downtown Pittsburgh, Pennsylvania, with the suburban area. Three rivers —the Allegheny, Monongahela, and Ohio—join at the famous "Golden Triangle."

A Dream Becomes a Reality

Every bridge starts as an idea. Someone believes that a bridge can be built where there has never been one before. Or perhaps an older bridge has to be replaced with a newer and better one. Then bridge designers and engineers set to work to solve the problems. *Add* ~~that~~ *Sandak says in his book, Bridges, that*

In planning a bridge, engineers must consider many things. Engineers find out the number and kinds of vehicles that will use the bridge. They study the width and depth of the water. They learn whether the surrounding land is marshy, rocky, or sandy and what the river bottom is like.

The designer must decide what the different parts of a bridge will be made of. They may be stone or concrete, steel or other metals. Bridges are usually made from a combination of these. *(1989)*

Changes in temperature can be a problem in bridge building. Most materials expand when they are heated and shrink when they get cooler. Expansion joints are built into bridges. An expansion joint is a small gap in the bridge's structure that allows parts next to each other to shrink or swell a small amount.

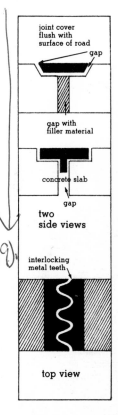

Types of Expansion Joints

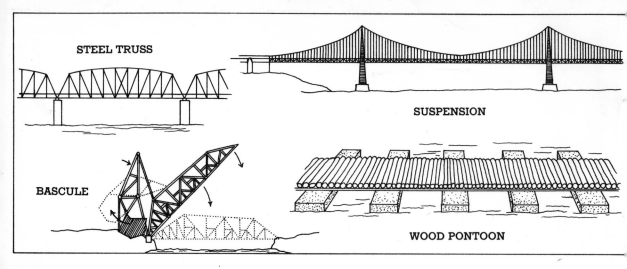

STEEL TRUSS

SUSPENSION

BASCULE

WOOD PONTOON

Some Types of Bridges
A bridge needs to be strong enough to stand up to flood waters, shipping accidents, and the wear caused by weather and chemicals in the air. And bridges must be able to withstand high winds. Even a light wind can set up forces that may rip the cables loose from a suspension bridge that is poorly designed. In 1940 the Tacoma Narrows Bridge in Washington began to twist in a 42-mph (67-kph) wind. The roadway was torn from its hangers and collapsed into the churning waters below.

Engineers must decide what kind of bridge will best fit specific needs. There are many kinds of bridges, but they may all be classed either as **fixed** or **movable**. All bridges are variations of three basic types: **beam**, **arch**, and **suspension**.

Beam bridges can be simple deck slabs or elaborate **trusswork** structures. One kind of beam bridge is called a **cantilever**. It must be specially supported and balanced to be strong.

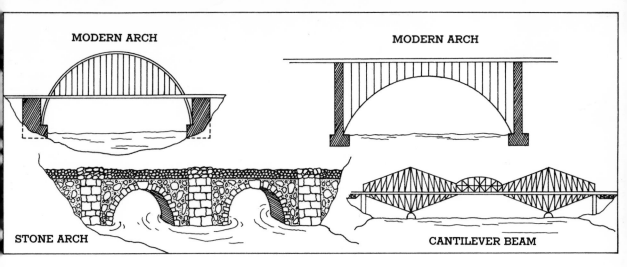

MODERN ARCH   MODERN ARCH

STONE ARCH   CANTILEVER BEAM

Arch bridges may be built from stone or
concrete. Or they may be complex steel structures.

Suspension bridges have strong wire cables that
hold up the roadway.

Sometimes the completed bridge is a
combination of the basic types. Piers may support
cantilever sections while a gap between the
cantilevers may be spanned by a truss section.
Combination bridges are often used to span bays
or wide rivers.

Since 1964 travel time across
Chesapeake Bay has been shortened
by the 17½-mile (28 km)
Chesapeake Bay Bridge-Tunnel.
It is a combination of bridge
sections, shown here, and
underwater tunnels.

BRIDGE FOUNDATIONS

A bridge needs to be strong. All parts of a bridge work together to make a structure that will hold itself up and carry the people and vehicles that use the bridge. A bridge's strength must be built in from the bottom up.

The section of roadway that leads from the land to the bridge is called the **approach**. The roadway itself is often called the **deck** of the bridge. **Abutments** are the supports on which the bridge structure rests at each end. Abutments are usually built on land.

The supports between the abutments are called **piers**. A section of a bridge between piers is called a **span**. Piers sometimes stand on dry land or are built to extend down through the water to solid ground, or **bedrock**.

A pier is usually a mass of concrete or rock. Iron, concrete, or timber **piles** may be driven into

Parts of a Bridge

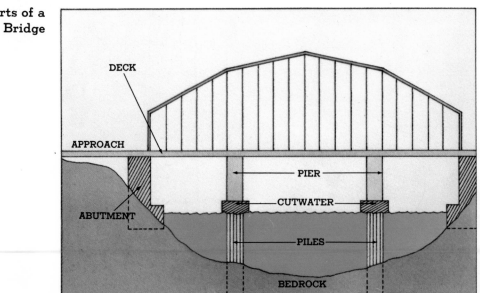

soft ground to give firmness to the piers built on top. Piers are often covered with hard stone or steel to keep water from wearing them away.

If a pier stands in the water, its base often has a **cutwater** built around it. A cutwater is a protective steel or stone collar that looks like a little island or boat. The cutwater keeps water from washing the pier away. It also saves the pier from damage if a boat runs into it.

Building the foundation of a bridge in and around a riverbed is a difficult task. There are ways to keep bridge builders safe and dry as they do their dangerous work.

Cofferdams are built down to the bottom of the water. These are wooden or steel walls or frameworks that make round or rectangular boxes. Concrete is poured inside the cofferdams to form the piers.

Where the water is very deep or the riverbed is very soft, **caissons** may be needed to build the piers. Caissons are watertight boxes or cylinders. Some kinds of caissons allow people to work underwater. Air pressure inside the caisson keeps water out. Air is trapped so that workers can dig pier foundations. A weighted caisson, resting on a river bottom, sinks farther down as digging continues. When it reaches the desired depth, the caisson can be filled with concrete. Then the top of the caisson becomes a solid base for a pier.

A cofferdam

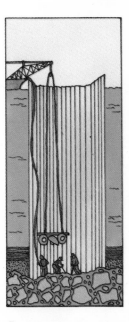
An open caisson

13

FINISHING THE BRIDGE

After the foundations and supports are in place, the roadway and its supports must be completed. This upper part, or **superstructure,** may be finished by one of several different methods.

Staging. This involves building a complete wooden framework and then erecting the bridge around it.

Cantilevering Out. This means building the bridge out from the ends in toward the center. Strong cables support the bridge parts until the bridge is complete.

"Cantilevering out," or joining the two sections of the Grand Island Bridge, near Buffalo, New York.

Rolling Out. The sections of the bridge are assembled on land and then rolled out on wheels over the gap and positioned on the piers. This method works only for bridges that have flat, straight decks.

Floating Out. This is a method in which huge sections are floated into the river channel on barges. They are then hoisted into place.

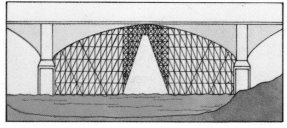

STAGING

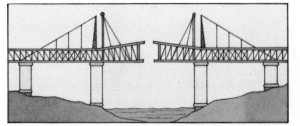

CANTILEVERING OUT

ROLLING OUT

FLOATING OUT

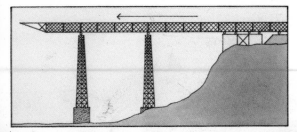

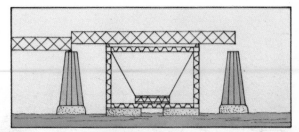

Beam Bridges

A beam bridge is the most basic type of bridge. A tree that falls across a stream and connects both banks is a simple beam bridge. Other simple beam bridges use straight, flat boards or slabs. These slabs can span only a short distance between two supports. With more supports, a beam bridge can span a greater distance.

Beam bridges are usually low, and there is only a narrow opening between the piers. Most large ships cannot pass under beam bridges.

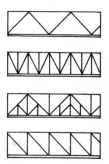

TRUSS BRIDGES

A **truss** bridge is a beam bridge made up of triangles. Truss bridges get their strength from the rigidity of the triangle. Sometimes the triangle is divided with an upright support, called a **king post**. This gives it added strength.

Many of the covered bridges built in America about 200 years ago were wooden truss bridges with roofs over them. Roofs gave the bridges protection and strength.

Left: an early railroad bridge, built entirely of wood. *Right:* a modern girder bridge supported by truss sections.

Early bridges were made from wood. They were cheap and easy to build, but they could only stand up to light traffic. Wood also catches fire easily and can rot quickly.

In the middle of the 1800s, iron was sometimes used to build bridges. Iron bridges could not catch fire, but they were not much stronger than wooden ones. Some railroad bridges were made of iron, but many of them collapsed under the weight of trains. In 1879, more than eighty people on a British passenger train were killed when the Tay Bridge in Scotland crumbled.

At about the same time, new processes made steelmaking easier and cheaper. Finally, the perfect material for making stronger and longer-lasting bridges had been discovered. Engineers, from their past experiences, quickly learned how to make the best use of steel.

A group of modern steel girder bridges. In the foreground, a footbridge leads up to a larger bridge. In the background is a highway overpass bridge.

GIRDER BRIDGES

Most American highway bridges are **girder** bridges. Straight steel beams are laid across abutments and are decked with concrete slabs. These beams are called girders. This is a good building method for bridges less than 100 feet (30 m) in length. Longer girder bridges with spans up to 700 feet (210 m) are often decked with steel plates. Girder bridges that carry railway traffic have extra steel crossbeams.

CANTILEVER BRIDGES

A cantilever bridge is a kind of beam bridge. It is usually built in two sections, which extend out from each bank. Each section is something like a diving board, or like a bracket on a bookshelf. Each end supports itself and the sections meet in the middle. The cantilever must be carefully balanced and counterbalanced. It has to be firmly

The Huey Long Bridge crosses the Mississippi River at New Orleans. It is a cantilever bridge.

anchored on each bank. Sometimes a gap is left between the cantilevers, and a section of beam, or a truss, is laid to connect the two.

Modern cantilever bridges are usually made up of huge steel trusses that are often roughly diamond-shaped, with a roadway passing through the middle. The truss is balanced so that underneath it rests on a single pier. Arms of the truss extend out and are joined so that they support each other.

Three sections of trusses form a typical cantilever bridge. An anchor span forms the bridge approach. It stretches from an end support on the bank to a tower. The tower or pier section has two arms or cantilevers that join with the anchor span on the bank and extend out toward the next cantilever.

The famous Quebec Bridge across the St. Lawrence River. The section in the middle, called a suspended span, links the two cantilever "arms."

Arch Bridges

Nobody knows who built the first arch. Perhaps someone copied a form found in nature—like the rounded entrance to a cave. The first kind of arch was a **corbeled**, or stepped, arch. It had rows of brick or stone piled on top of each other. Each row extended a little farther toward the middle until the rows met at the top. Later, rounded arches were made from wedge-shaped stones piled up the same way.

Arch bridges were built in Mesopotamia as long ago as 4000 B.C., and in Egypt around 3600 B.C. Remains of an ancient Roman arch bridge, the Ponte Rotto, still stand on the Tiber River in Rome.

There is an arch bridge in China that was built around A.D. 600 and is still in use today. The

Corbeled
Arch

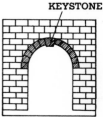

KEYSTONE

Rounded
Arch

The Ponte Sant'Angelo in Rome was built on the Tiber River by the Emperor Hadrian in A.D. 134.

The Pont du Gard is 900 feet (270 m) long. It was built in France by Roman engineers.

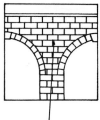

SPANDREL

Two modern steel arch bridges. *Left:* the Rainbow Bridge near Niagara Falls. *Right:* the Bayonne Bridge.

spandrels of the bridge have arched openings. These are both useful and attractive. When the water level rises, the openings allow water to pass through them.

The Romans invented special arch bridges to carry water. These are called aqueducts. The Pont du Gard carries water to the city of Nîmes, France. This aqueduct was built in 19 B.C., and is still in use today. Three tiers of arches rise 155 feet (46.5 m) into the air.

Arch bridges get their strength from the arch form itself. An arch is constructed from stone, brick or concrete. It must be supported by

scaffolding, called **falsework**, until the work is done. The falsework keeps the pieces in place until the arch is finished.

The arch is built curving in from the ends toward the middle. When the **keystone**, or topmost block, is in place, the arch can support itself and the falsework is removed.

MODERN STEEL ARCH BRIDGES

Today, many arch bridges are built from concrete that has been reinforced with networks of wire. Some modern arch bridges are built up from hollow concrete wedges.

In some cases, a steel arch forms a support to hold up the roadway above. This is similar in form to a stone arch bridge, although steel is in some ways a stronger material. Steel means that an arch bridge can be longer.

In other arch bridges, a huge steel arch spans the distance from shore to shore, or from pier to pier. The arch serves as a framework. Cables hang down from the arch to hold up the roadway. The Bayonne Bridge, between Staten Island and New Jersey, is one of the world's most famous steel arch bridges.

Suspension Bridges

Suspension bridges are the biggest and most exciting type of bridge. They can span the longest distances and soar the highest above the water.

A suspension bridge is the best type to build over a waterway that is used for navigation. The roadway of a suspension bridge can be so high in the air that even the largest ships can pass under it.

Primitive suspension bridges were built in Asia and South America many hundreds of years ago. Twisted fibers, vines, and pieces of bamboo held the narrow footpath of the bridge in place. Steel cable suspension bridges were first built in Great Britain in the early 1800s.

A suspension bridge is supported by cables strung between towers. First the piers are built.

Old and new suspension bridges. *Opposite:* the Mackinac Bridge, built in 1957. *Left:* a primitive Chinese suspension bridge.

Then large concrete and steel towers are built on top of the piers. The towers may rise hundreds of feet in the air. The towers help support the approaches to the bridge. The cables loop down between the towers.

The main cables must be fastened on the banks in secure **anchorings**. The ends of the cables are embedded in concrete and the anchorings are usually fastened to solid rock. It is important that they never come loose, because the cables would fall down and the bridge would collapse.

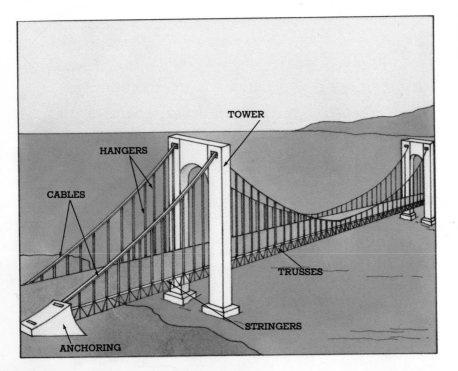

Parts of a Suspension Bridge

TOWER

HANGERS

CABLES

TRUSSES

STRINGERS

ANCHORING

23

A section of the George Washington Bridge showing hangers that are strung down from the main cables. They support the roadway.

The placement of the cable begins by workers passing wire ropes between the two banks and looping the wire ropes over the tops of the towers. A footbridge called a **catwalk** serves as a platform.

Then individual wires are strung. A device called a spider moves back and forth over the wires, "spinning" threadlike wires into the cable. Slowly the cable gets thicker and thicker.

Powerful pincers press the wires tightly together and bind them with still more wire to make each large cable. A doughnut-shaped machine wraps galvanized wire around the cables to protect them from the weather. Usually the cable is wrapped with a layer of lead or stainless steel bands for further protection.

Sections of truss keep the cables the same distance apart and make a framework for the roadway. **Stringers**—large steel beams—are placed across the trusses. These form the foundation of the deck or roadbed. The road is laid on top of this framework.

One of the world's most famous suspension bridges was one hundred years old in 1983.

When the Brooklyn Bridge opened in 1883, its stone towers made it the tallest structure in North America. At that time, it was one and a half times longer than any other suspension bridge in the world. It was important because so many bridge-building techniques were being used for the first time. Now much longer and more delicate suspension bridges are built.

Two views of the Brooklyn Bridge. *Left:* as it appeared in 1883. *Right:* as it looks a hundred years later.

The Verrazano-Narrows Bridge was built over the entrance to New York City's harbor between Brooklyn and Staten Island. Completed in 1964, it took seventy years of planning and six years of actual construction. It is 4,260 feet (1,299 m) long.

The Verrazano-Narrows Bridge under construction. The towers are 2 inches (5 cm) farther apart at the top than at the bottom. This is because of the curve of the earth's surface. It is one of the longest suspension bridges in the world.

Movable Bridges

A movable bridge is built in a place where a bridge is needed most of the time. But sometimes a part of that bridge can be moved. There are several types of bridges that move in different ways, usually to let boats sail through a channel.

BASCULE BRIDGES

A **drawbridge** is a kind of **bascule bridge**. Tower Bridge, in London, England, is an example of a bascule bridge. The movable roadway section can be lifted or lowered in four minutes.

Bascule means "seesaw" in French. And a bascule bridge operates very much like a seesaw. Single-leaf or double-leaf bascules usually have heavy concrete weights. These weights counterbalance the weight of the spans that reach out over the water. Motors make the weights go down to lift the spans of the bridge.

Two bascule bridges. *Left:* London's famous Tower Bridge. *Right:* a drawbridge that has been opened to let a ship pass through.

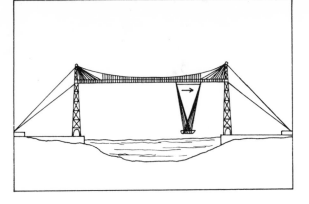

A drawing of a transporter bridge in Rouen, France. The suspended cable car carries passengers from one side to the other.

TRANSPORTER BRIDGE

A transporter is an unusual kind of movable bridge. It is often used over areas where water traffic is heavy and road traffic is light. It is like a bridge and cable car combined. A steel framework holds the tracks for a car that can carry passengers and freight. Cables pull the car from one bank to the other.

VERTICAL LIFT BRIDGE

A vertical lift bridge works like an elevator. The roadway is attached to two columns and is continuous. When a ship needs to pass underneath it, a system of cables and pulleys lifts the roadway high above the normal level.

Two vertical lift bridges. At left, the roadway is closed. At right, the roadway has been lifted to let ship traffic through.

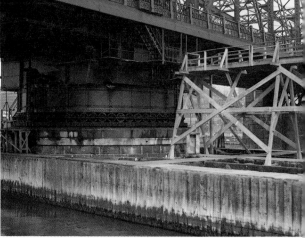

Left: a railroad swing bridge opens to let a steamer through. *Right:* small notched wheels turn a large drumlike wheel to swing the bridge open.

SWING BRIDGE

A swing bridge has a movable section of roadway built on a huge drumlike support. Wheels can turn this section of roadway at a right angle. This opens a channel that allows boats to pass through.

ROLLING, OR RETRACTABLE, BRIDGE

This is a rare type of movable bridge. It allows the span to move away from its opening on wheels or rollers.

PONTOON BRIDGE

The armies of ancient Persia first used **pontoon bridges**. They laid planks between small boats. Or sometimes they inflated and then sealed animal skins. Filled with air, the skins would float.

Because pontoon bridges can be put up quickly, they have been important in war. But they can also be destroyed easily, and few of them have been permanent.

When a pontoon bridge is built today, metal cylinders or hollow concrete boxes are filled with

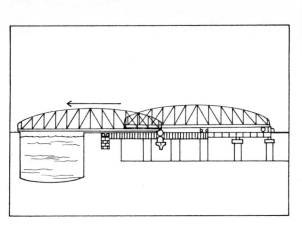

air. Like the animal skins of long ago, they will also float. Or the concrete boxes can be attached to permanent piers or fixed supports.

In 1940, a permanent pontoon bridge was built on Lake Washington in Seattle, Washington. It is more than 2 miles (3.2 km) long. Twenty-five pontoons were made of hollow concrete. These hold up the roadway. A sliding section 200 feet (60 m) long can be moved to make a channel for ships.

Left: a drawing of a rolling bridge in England. *Right:* a World War II pontoon bridge. It was put up quickly to replace a bridge destroyed by retreating soldiers.

Bridges Today and Tomorrow

In the future, longer and more daring bridges will be built. Suspension bridges will have spans many miles long. Places that now can be reached only by boat or ferry will be linked by bridges. In the world of bridges, builders will be limited only by their imaginations.

Words About Bridges

Abutment. The main support at each end of a bridge. The sides that support an arch are also called abutments.

Anchoring. The place where the cables of a suspension bridge are firmly fastened on land. Anchorings are often embedded in concrete.

Anchor span. The land end of a cantilever bridge.

Approach. A section of roadway leading to a bridge.

Aqueduct. An arched bridge used for carrying water.

Bascule bridge. A type of movable bridge that allows a section or sections to be lifted like a seesaw.

Beam bridge. The simplest type of bridge. It consists of a straight section across two supports.

Bedrock. Hard, solid rock underneath layers of earth or mud.

Caisson. A watertight, hollow chamber used for underwater construction.

Cantilever. A way of building by suspending a beam or bracket that is supported at one end only.

Cofferdam. A boxlike temporary dam often used in bridge building.

Corbeled arch. A stepped arch with each row of brick or stone extending a little further toward the middle than the row beneath it.

Deck. The road surface of a bridge.

Drawbridge. A movable bridge.

Falsework. A framework supporting an arch that is under construction.

Fixed bridge. A type of bridge that always remains in place. It has no movable parts.

Girder. A large beam.

Hangers. Smaller cables that support the roadway of a suspension bridge.

King post. An upright support dividing the triangle of a truss.

Movable bridge. A bridge with movable parts that can change position to allow the passage of water traffic.

Piers. The undersupports of a bridge.

Piles. Columns of wood, metal, or concrete placed in the ground to give stability and support.

Pontoon bridge. A bridge supported on floating platforms or boats.

Rolling, or retractable, bridge. A movable bridge that can be rolled out of the water.

Span. A section of bridge between two piers.

Spandrel. A triangular area around the curve of an arch.

Staging. A way of building a bridge using a complex framework.

Stringers. Large steel beams that help support the roadway of a suspension bridge.

Superstructure. The portion of a bridge above the waterline and foundations.

Suspension bridge. A type of bridge supported on huge steel cables.

Swing bridge. A movable bridge with a central section of roadway that can swing around to open up a channel.

Towers. The tall upright supports that hold up the main cables of a suspension bridge.

Transporter. A rare kind of movable bridge for carrying passengers or freight. It is usually like a cable car.

Truss. A framework made up of triangular parts.

Vertical lift bridge. A movable bridge that lifts the roadway straight up with pulleys and cables.

Viaduct. A bridge that carries a roadway over land.

Index